Fawn and Freeze:

A Debut Collection of Poems By

Elizabeth Gade

*this collection contains scenes of graphic nature, which could be triggering to survivors

Dedicated to my daughter, the bravest most creative soul I know. I love you.

Christine &
keep shining
bright!
—Elizabeth Gade

POET · SURVIVOR · ADVOCATE ·

Elizabeth Gade

@ELIZABETHGADETHEPOET

Table Of Contents

Remove My Abuser…page 4
An Open Letter To My Fellow Survivors…page 7
The Radicalization…page 11
The Disappearance…page 14
Abigail…page 17
Whipping Girls…page 21
Theft Of Property…page 24
Tried To Be Good…page 27
Body Of Mine…page 30
A Pimp Named Moses…page 33
Why I Didn't Leave…page 34
The Body Of The Lamb…page 36
Fallen…page 37
trick…page 47
What PTSD Feels Like…page 49
My Darling Daughter…page 50
Gluttony…page 56
No Human Involved…page 58
The Letting Go…page 60
The Offering…page 62
The Blood Came…page 65
Thirsting…page 67
Woman Who Glows In The Dark…page 70
Blooming…page 72
Sister…page 74

Remove My Abuser

~~Abused woman~~
madwoman with a vision
driven by the brutality
that forged me

the blade of
trauma pressed
against my
throat

remove my abuser
and the abuse has
programmed me
to abuse
myself

this is the double edged
sword

the steel trap of the

mind

splitting not as a

symptom

but as a way to save me

from myself

if the core of all that is good

is hidden

it can not be

shattered or destroyed

I gave you

my body

my mind

my language

the best choice parts of me

in between

but the very essence of me

the core of all that is good
the part you underestimated

the soft underbelly
of my celestial animal self

was saved

nurtured
nourished
empowered

and it's all coming back to
me.

An Open Letter To My Fellow Survivors:

You are not the

house of horrors

trauma built

inside of

you

they tried to fit us

into cheap hotel rooms

and jail cells and

locked wards

of hospitals

slapped us with labels

the same way your abuser

first slapped you across

the face

and you ceased to be you

in one skin splitting

split second

as the mind splits

to wall off the trauma

Don't bleed on the good carpet

It takes courage

to look beyond

medical records

or a prison number

and see

your own humanity

in a society

that will weaponize

your trauma

against

you

never let you up
off your knees

shame you back
to your abuser

police your body

What were you wearing
Did you keep your legs shut

this is the wound of being born
woman we all
carry

this is the price to pay
for daring
to embody

Goddess

Woman

Whore

Witch

Crone

for allowing just the smallest spark

of the divine feminine

to shine through

never stop fighting

for you

for your right

to be the bravest woman

you've ever

incarnated

and to see her

in all the women

you'll ever

meet

The Radicalization

My trauma radicalized me
made my boundaries
impossible to ignore

made me harder to
~~love~~
manipulate

created a version of me
that is raw and loud
unable to fix my face
in compliance

killed everything inside of me
that was meek

I had to fight
for my softness back

fight or die
fight or submit

there is no submission left

pillaged by trauma
fractured bones picked
clean

there is a war inside of me

and healing allows
for no compromise

this is an act of
rebellion

the digging of secrets from
your carcass

the choosing of

Self

at all costs

this is how my trauma

radicalized me

these are the gifts

this is

me

The Disappearance

I mastered the art of the

disappearance act

but could never

remove me

from myself

the worthlessness that followed

from birth

the weight of being born

woman

I've never met

anyone

as insatiable

as me

only mountains could house

this type of frenzied

loathing of

self

women slept the war out of men

and buried their own rage

in rose beds

leeched it into bone

marrow broth

I birthed this poem

the first time a man split my skin

with his fist

trauma doesn't make you stronger

it crushes

buries

all the best parts of you

makes despair

a tangible taste in your mouth

you can't

wash

out

it made my body

inhospitable

the disappearance

of me

gradual

Abigail

You are more than

my mirror

diagnosis

trading personality

labels

like playing cards

The broken brain club

you are the most

in depth

reflection

of all that is good

in me

you are the lighthouse

that withstands the gnashing winds

of my trauma

we have both
struggled to breathe
pressed spine down

carved herringbone
silvered slivered scars
into our skin

but this is not
a trauma bond

this is a coming home

a shutting of doors
on the outside world

the tiny span of your palm
on my back

a safe haven

from shame

the sharp furnaced edges

of hipbone

a twitching velvet

nose

a shuttered sapphic place

where women use their mouths

and voices and hands

redefining boundaries of self

we have been

awash with intimacy

and I let the wave

of you

carry me into the future

this beastly

human experience

made bearable

by you

this love

is an anchoring

I carry you

rooted into

me

Whipping Girls

Could not good girl
my way to safety

could not fawn
my way out of the
lion's den

inside every woman
is the need to exist
beyond the proximity
of men

behind every mediocre man
is his own personal
whipping girl

Could not talk therapy
my way through it

had to wade

waist deep through

the darkness my abusers

left behind

there is work to be done

mining the murky depths

of my subconscious

I am nothing

if not a

warrior

war shipped

woman

from the Magdalene

bloodlines we rise

serpent hipped

open lipped

to manifest

this poem is a
battle cry

the victory song of
women rising,

transcending

Theft Of Property

They said I was
a whore
before I'd even
kissed a boy

And so it was

weaponized my body
against me

molded me into a
container for
men

bastardized Eve
villainized Medusa

distorted the meaning
of virgin

robbed us of our

sexual agency

pillaged our wombs

for generations

of wounding

declared rape

not as a crime

against women

but the theft of property

from men

Dress codes won't protect you

crushed us under

boot heels

tried to hang us

from history

yet we are the origin

of creation,

impossible to tame

the universe conspires

in our favor,

rising up to meet

the divine feminine

over and over

lifetime after lifetime

Tried To Be Good

What if healing
and sobriety
was not something we
white knuckled into submission

but instead a slow unfurling

slow, slower

a patient cultivation of
sacred space
any place we dare
show up
broken but authentic

self-acceptance as a radical act of love

my embodiment of this
human experience is limitless

starkly flawed

I tried to be good. Had to settled for being wild and seen.

I carry this wildness into
the world
dragging it behind me like an anchor
was never white flag material

I make space on the yoga mat
and inside my heart
learn to lay boundaries
like fences
tend to myself first even when
it feels strange and foreign

I love you but I can never call you again

I am becoming
the woman
I showed up to be all those

lifetimes ago

I died a thousand deaths
to be this woman
one who chooses herself
every time
no matter the cost

A stand alone
scream from the soul
type of woman

she is free

Body Of Mine

This poem is for my body
what anchors me to this earth
keeps me grounded in this world

my most hated possession
what holds all my hate and resentment
stores all the trauma

works even when I'm tired
and I haven't told it
thank you
or
I love you

in a very long time

maybe it's been forever

since I allowed my body

rest and appreciation

this beautifully wretched
body of mine
prone to decay
and destruction

how many days
borrowed against time

how many favors owed

and still it persists
this body of mine

even as it's undervalued
and overused

viewed as mundane

this poem is for my body

a recognition

olive branch finally extending

I see you body

and it's an

honor

to call you mine

I invite you

body to come

and sit

still with me

to be

with me

body of mine

the meeting of Self

A Pimp Named Moses

the clean wet split of pistol against skull

as the red sea parts inside of me

whores know god too

we spend our lives on our knees

praying

who do you think we call out for

what's the difference between

a pimp and a pastor preaching

I can't tell

their number one commandment

is the same

put the fear of god in her

Why I Didn't Leave

I was infatuated. I was trauma bonded after being love bombed. I was isolated. I was scared for my life. I didn't think anyone would believe me. I thought I deserved it. I didn't want another victim to take my place. I was invisible. I was broken down. I was shattered. I had no sense of self. I was brainwashed. It's everywhere. It's a bigger network than you could imagine. I thought I could leave at first. I couldn't leave. It was my fault. I didn't want to die. I didn't want my family to die. I believed him. I didn't think anyone could ever love me after what I had lived through. I couldn't love myself. There were eyes everywhere. There was nowhere to run to. No human involved. Dead hooker jokes. Society says I'm worthless and I deserved it. It's what girls like me get. I was an empty shell. I was good at it. I was a robot. I thought I could pay my way out but no amount was enough. I wanted to die. I feared the guns. I believed I was going to die every time he beat me. I lived in fear 24/7. It's the most primal emotion. My mental functions eroded. The hotels were complacent, sometimes accomplices. My brain disassociated weeks and months to protect me. My brain tried to protect me from the trauma. My brain created parts. Some parts were loyal to him. Most parts were loyal to him. Those parts told on myself. I wasn't allowed thoughts of my own. There was no planning. There was no hiding. Leaving and getting caught was so much worse. Once I jumped out a moving car. I interacted with the police over and over throughout the years. No one helped me. I didn't think I'd live past 30 years of age anyways. I couldn't see past a minute, an hour, a day. There was nowhere to run. I became a part of him. There was no self. I was a parrot. I tried my best. I stayed alive. I stayed alive. I stayed alive.

The Body Of The Lamb

They take away our names and we answer to whatever
they call us. I know the color of her hair and the size of
skirt she wore but I don't know if she made it out alive.
If she ever made it home. Do any of us make it home?
Do you remember? These are the things I wish I could
remember. The last time someone spoke the name my
mother gave me. The last time someone I loved touched
my body gently. The last holiday I celebrated. The last
hug I received. Do you remember? In the beginning I let
myself remember, but eventually life before fades. The
years swallow me whole. There is no before. There is
only today, right now, this moment. This pain. This
desperation, the animal sickness in the belly. The silent
mouth that opens to man, to body, the last communion,
the slick steel, the chaliced revolver. You try not to look
in the mirror because she is no longer here. You sent her
away, but she never made it home. There was no place to
go. You are her. The body. The name. I am you. The
head that bows. I am here. The pale flanked lamb,
broken and begging.

Fallen

center stage

legs spread

center of the bed

hardened edges soften

in the flickering ambiance

of a dozen lit candles

spotlighted

as I stroke the vulnerable underside

of his exposed male ego

lost in a scented

haze of sweat

hot wax and

expensive

perfume

the heat of his palm

threatens to burn down

the small

of my back

and I press against

the cool metal contrast

of his

wedding ring

we both thirst

we both seek relief

of a different nature

coating the insides

of our mouths with champagne

that foams and fizzes

but quenches nothing

I open to them

these men staking their claim

but still naive to so many

shut doors

inside of me

that bar their entrance

buried in soft flesh

sinking life

bare feet

caught

in shifting sand

they imprint my skin

with a multitude

of smudged fingerprints

my soul

smeared like a dirty

windowpane

I watch

as he moves over me

and I take flight

traveling

to find solace

in solitude filled places of my past

he's here

but in my mind

I'm walking softly down

pine needle carpeted paths

Eve paved the way

generations

of fallen women

whores and harlots

cast out of the garden

stigmatized by

society

political perversions

when prosecuted by the same

public figures who pay

for it on the sly

flesh of the apple

replaced

by the temptation of

cold hard

cash

invisible

important parts

of my inner self

sold

unable to get

back

men took

but I gave too feely

everyone has a price

and I've paid mine

mistress

of the moment

well-kept and compensated

by the hour

a perfectly coifed

hollow shell

of my

former

self

well versed

in current events

and proper table manners

but unable to speak

my mind

brittle smile

breaking

I wait for the rising tide

of my oil laced bathwater

to wash away

all traces

of him

unclean currency

counted by the hundreds

and stuffed into a plain white envelope

mocks me from the marble topped

bathroom counter

and leaves me

feeling

counterfeit

outside my window

is a dazzling display

a modern day mirage

swathed

in a velvet gown of darkness

the heaving bosom of this city

that never sleeps

necklaced

in glittering gaudy lights

reminding me that

even the most beautiful

man-made stars

fail

burn out and

fall

shattering

on the dirty pavement

29 stories below

what is there left to lose

besides love

already bought

and paid

for

trick

the fishbones in the throat
the truth that won't make its way out

admit you only want women as a commodity
or not at all

the body always has a price
it's the soul you can do without

you looked me in the eyes
still you couldn't see my humanity

I became a mirror
for my survival

while I protected you
from your goddamn self

there was no rescue

I saved myself

but first I had to trick
myself into believing

I was worth
saving

\

What PTSD Feels Like

It feels like a bomb went off inside of me. It feels like I
went through a war. I am shattered buildings and fire
scorched earth. I have a thousand horror movies playing
inside my head and I'm the star of them all. In my
dreams I am always brought back. Returned to appease
the monster, over and over. I can never run fast enough. I
can never outrun it or outdrink it or outfuck it. It's the
shadow that forever looms. It's the isolation in the eye of
a storm. It's a two way mirror I can see out of, but they
can never see in. No one can ever see me. It's the shame
that comes in waves. It's the *shame*. It's how my brain
punishes me for talking about it. I deserved it. It feels
like I'm drowning when I'm breathing. It's believing I
don't deserve to breathe. I'm just trying to breathe
through this. I can't breathe. I can't breathe. I can't
breathe.

My Darling Daughter

I have been locked up 269 days
and you, my darling daughter
are only 236 days old.

When the math is done
it cquals 33 days you spent
imprisoned in my womb
while I was incarcerated behind
cinderblock jailhouse walls.

My constant companion,
my inner strength,
I had nothing to offer
beyond the sound of my voice,
reading you surah's from the Quran
morning and night.

I swear, my darling daughter
I cherished every moment
we had together.

When that Spring day came
I labored away the afternoon
under the watchful eyes of two female
correction officers, an army of nurses
flanking the bed but no
familiar faces in sight,
your father banished
to wait in the hospital lobby
because security trumps
the comfort of family
every time.

A first time mother,
slick with sweat,
shivering in fear,
reduced to instinct like
every other animal birthing
that Spring,
bearing down until finally
my body gave way and
you slipped from between
my thighs like a gift.

I'll never forget the surprising
weight of you on my chest,

all 8 pounds 2 ounces of you,
how you looked so much like your father,
the way you laid there eerily silent
until I spoke to you in Arabic
and your response was
a lusty cry that severed
my heart into two
separate halves.

The doctor mended torn flesh
as the guard cuffed one ankle
to the bed and I, I just held you.

You, my darling daughter
are my favorite season.

You are morning dew
and cleansing rains,
clear blue skies
and new beginnings.

I cradled you in my arms for 48 hours straight,
nursed you at my breast, memorized
your perfect little face until
I was forced to swaddle you
one last time, lay you gently
in the arms of a nurse
and submit to being
led away in shackles.

I swear, my darling daughter
I went back to that jail in despair,
an empty shell of myself,
a body with no purpose,
a mother without her child.

Now two full seasons have past,
as I write this poem
it's been 234 days
since I've held you last
and all around the leaves
on the trees are dying
and inside me all hope
has begun to fall away.

What good is a day spent
locked behind this cell door
while my child is asleep
in her crib four states away.

When asked if I have children
my mouth says *I am a mother*
but my insides are screaming
I am a mother who hasn't
been given a chance
*to **be** a mother*.

Comfort is hard to find
in a handful of memories
and well-meaning pictures
of how much you've grown
when all that I remember
is overshadowed by
everything I have lost,
everything I have missed,
everything I cannot get back.

I swear, my darling daughter
I miss you with every atom of my heart,
I miss you with an aching desperation,
I miss you like a person drowning

misses their last gasping
breath of air.

Winter lays her icy fingers against my cheek,
it's the beginning of another season
spent away from you,
another day locked up,
suspended in time,
waiting for Spring.

Gluttony

I am a glutton

for

punishment

crammed my mouth

full

of all the lies

you told me

beat into me

only to be left

choking

on my own

self-worth

hungry for ~~me~~

more

why am I always
left

wanting

that's not my
appetite
it's insatiable

that's a black hole
inside of me
that obliterates
love

and all sense
of self-respect

your last parting
gift

No Human Involved

The trauma screams
you don't matter
you were never supposed to
survive

much less open your mouth
and speak

the trauma was supposed to silence you
grind you into dust; spit you out

I am nothing but a science experiment
what happens when you
obliterate
her entire sense of Self

no human involved

we don't say that anymore

but the trauma says

eventually

there's nothing left
to break anymore

The Letting Go

Skin taunt like over ripe fruit
velveteen under your mouth
the way it eventually

yields
and splits
wetly

against the guillotine
of your teeth

I yield to your sharp edges

I yield
I yield

there is an opening
in the cosmic imprint of time
and I fall through

burrow beneath the

layers of

gristle and flesh

the tendons strung tight

as your mania

the muffled drum

of womb and pumping blood

the silence between us

threatens to untether me

I'm left grasping for roots

that never took

just your warmed flesh

and thick fingers

fishhook pressed against

slippery pubic

bone

pinned and gasping

I let go

The Offering

The clouds cathedral around the mountain

as surely as my body revolves

around this forest

like clockwork

like the most committed lover

or the sinners who kneel in the pews

every Sunday

I drag my heaviness into the trees

the desert

the ragged peaks

I've offered up the basin

of my hipbones

to the Sun

let the air touch

naked skin

like nervous moist fingers

the ant crawls along my collarbone
as the shuffling leaves beg
for my attention

let me live in this moment forever
body suspended between moss and bark

let me forget about the seasons
of living; thrashing
like an animal caught in a trap

trying to breathe in a twisted habitat
of steel and cement
grime and noise

forehead pressed to windowpane
while the city growls back at me
better the monster you know
than the devil you don't

you learn the predators like the back of your hand

how they feast and the way they move

twigs snap

bones break

and still the body

is brought back to this forest

to hike

to observe

to revel in the cruelty of nature

and my place in it

The Blood Came

The blood came before
the rain did

the poems came before
the healing arrived

the trauma
the trauma

has always been
with its snapping frenzied jaws

I never belonged anywhere
the girl who thrived in chaos

prayed to god to make me anything
but dirty

daughter of Eve

flesh of the original sin

the shame

the shame

that serpentine scaled spiral

ends here

Thirsting

In the water of summer
the trees hurt
longing to be touched

calling out for us to put down
our laptops and cell phones
to stop flinging our bodies
full speed at computer chips
and stranger's hips

the mountain is calling and I must go
warrior woman pirate souled and hyena hearted
I dare you to love each other's
rebel soul

air your dirty laundry beautifully
send the skeletons in your closet on a spa day
hold a peace summit to share
the first time you
were ever called a whore or a slut

spare a moment of your time to

hug the homeless and look them in the eye

as you pass them your spare change

hold hands with yourself

in between relationships

pine is for endurance

in your absence I bring my body

to the trees and bathe my spirit

in peace can you imagine

a sacred former prostitute

hugging knotted trunks

and kissing fire scorched bark

rubbing fingers against

the perfect tear drop

of amber sap

asking to be filled again

download me with the innate knowledge

of my own inner wisdom

bind my wounds

as I struggle to stitch

up paper cuts

from my paper city

before I'm bled dry

the salve in my own salvation

has always been made inside

yes I am thirsting and hurting

but my body must make the journey with me as well

as I travel to the inner silence with no fear

of what I find amongst Self

Woman Who Glows In The Dark

I want the power to face beauty

and not look away

I want to say yes

and believe I deserve it

trauma says

stay small

turn away

isolate

you don't belong

every day is a

decision to face it

and not drown in the fear

to come out

the mud

bloom

where I stand

today

a woman who

glows in the dark

Blooming

Some days are easy
and some days are exhausting

the days you have to dig through the muck inside
take more hits than a heavyweight prize fighter
cling to life with mud between your fingers

I tend to rip
myself from situations
root first

but uprooted and
free aren't the same thing

what is blooming but an
unraveling

the loosening of petals

a joyous movement, a quiet consistency

an unfolding full of forward momentum

(an aching)

from whole

to empty

and back again

Sister

sister
we come from the north country
the cold country
on the border of another nation
each born into bracing winter winds
our narrow world isolated
insulated with blankets of brittle snow
we learned to breath in that frigid air
learned to swallow the bitterness
carried all the clichés of
dysfunctional family
and failed marriages
out into the world,
strengthened our insides
on all that icy indifference

sister
we were born five years apart

but equal in our long limbs

and matching pale blue eyes

able to see clearly

everything in front of us

everything we did not want out of life

the injustice of being born to our surroundings steeped in

ignorance

knowing we were destined for greatness

strong in the mind

you the scholar, the steady one

the stand-in mother, the mentor

me the poet, the unpredictable one

but predictable in my

own wild ways

sister

we are still children in my mind

still growing up at the end

of long dusty dirt roads

sweat of horses drying on our thighs

galloping hard across open fields

untainted by fear of falling

free from the expectations

of mothers and men

still years away from our own

self- imposed attempts of perfection,

of adulthood,

of my brilliant execution of failure

perfect in its own way,

before you were forced to play mediator

kept in limbo between our

self-created family war

the peacekeeper caught

behind enemy lines

white flag extended in vain

sister

we separated at the seams

our hands torn apart like the careless

ripping of paper dolls

the day you went out into the world

paving the way

oh how I envied your freedom

mourned the loss of you

sister friend confidant

the stone, the stability of my childhood

my secret aspiration

I wanted to be when I grew up

the first time I felt left behind

a stranger in my own family

sister

we were lost to each other along the way

you left first but I left farther and longer

hoping to be as brave and bold as you

a better older version of myself

instead I became the victim

of my self-imposed exile

tested the bonds of sisterhood

naïve to how you must have suffered

blood is thicker than water

but left untended

it becomes clotted and congealed

strangling the connection
allowing what we grew up believing
as unbreakable to rust and weaken
oh how we hurt the ones we love most
in our clumsy attempts at life

sister
we are together the best part of childhood
you are what grounds me to this world
the roots that sustain my family tree
the destination I have journeyed
long and hard towards
that place on a map
marked "home"

Acknowledgments

Many thanks to the following publications for first printing earlier versions of these poems: *The View Magazine, Other Worldly Women Press, The Elevation Review, Synkroniciti, 300 Days Of Sun, The Sober Girls Yoga Magazine, Progenitor, The Lindenwood Review, Nine Cloud Journal, Leo Literary Journal, MiniMag, Exist Otherwise, The GroundUp Publication, Gnashing Teeth Publication, A Room Of Her Own Foundation & La Palabra.*

To every pimp that pimped on me, and every client that bought me…I wish you healing so deep no other woman is ever hurt by you again.

To every survivor out there, from human trafficking and domestic violence and sexual assault, I see you and I love you. You are brave and kind and multifaced, but most of all you are enough. I pray you are surrounded by community and support. I pray you come to know yourself and love yourself no matter what. You are worthy.

To my own community of women, that has loved me through it all: Brook, Abby, Kristy, Nadia and Sonya I love you in this and every lifetime.

To the strong women in my family, my grandmother, my mom, my sisters, my aunties, my daughter I am here because of you.

To my new community I'm building: Kayleen, Michael, Crystal and Christina I appreciate you so much.

To Katrina Kaye and Jessica Helen Lopez, many thanks for beta reading and offering a blurb. To Zachary Kluckman, thank you for the help with formatting. You have all been such an inspiration to me on the way. Thank you to the entire Albuquerque poetry community for welcoming me and shaping my journey as a poet.

About The Author

Elizabeth Gade is a bisexual writer, human trafficking survivor and Certified Peer Recovery Specialist in the rural USA. As a human trafficking survivor, her lived experience of abuse and incarceration is what drives her to write and serve her community. She views writing as a radical way to connect with fellow survivors. Her poems have been published in The View Magazine, The Elevation Review, 300 Days of Sun, The Lindenwood Review, The Sober Girls Yoga Magazine, Exist Otherwise, MiniMag and many more. Elizabeth created LEO Literary Journal, an online journal dedicated to women writers affected by incarceration, addiction and/or domestic violence.
www.LeoLiteraryJournal.Weebly.com

She is also the creator and host of Survived To Write, a free survivor led writing circle on Zoom for human trafficking survivors of any gender 18+. Connect with her on Instagram @ElizabethGadeThePoet and @SurvivedToWrite

Made in the USA
Coppell, TX
31 March 2024

30722469R00046